Flaxseed Recipes

50 delicious recipes using Flaxseed to reduce weight and firing up your metabolism rate

Disclaimer

© Sarah Niles, 2014

No part of this eBook can be transmitted or reproduced in any form including print, electronic, photocopying, scanning, mechanical or recording without prior written permission from the author.

While the author has taken utmost efforts to ensure the accuracy of the written content, all readers are advised to follow information mentioned herein at their own risk. The author cannot be held responsible for any personal or commercial damage caused by misinterpretation of information. All readers are encouraged to seek professional advice when needed.

What You Will Find In This Book?

You all may be aware of the benefits that flaxseeds have but might not be aware of the interesting, delicious and easy ways to make yummy food that will reduce your weight and speed up your metabolism rate. Now isn't it exciting?

Flaxseed is high in omega-3 and is good for people with heart diseases, obesity, cholesterol problems and blood pressure. They are also helpful for patients with cancer.

Now you can keep a check on your weight and on what you eat by following simple recipes. In this book you will find:

1. How you can creatively make Flaxseed part of your daily cooking?
2. How you can derive tremendous benefits from Flaxseed that it has to offer?
3. Delicious recipes that can accommodate Flaxseed without ruing their taste.

The recipes in this book will tell you the amount of time required to cook and prepare any recipe. Al the recipes will use Flaxseed in one way or another. The aim of this book is to provide you scrumptious and appetizing ways to add flaxseed to your daily diet. All recipes come with serving size and cooking time. You can, therefore, choose the recipes according to your convenience of time and people you are serving.

It is however advised that you don't start using high amount of Flaxseed on your daily diet. They are extremely rich in fiber, proteins and other essential nutrients. Start with adding small amount of flaxseed to your diet and then gradually and slowly increasing.

This book will serve as a great guide towards healthy eating lifestyle and is worth your time and money.

Contents

- Disclaimer 2
- What You Will Find In This Book? 3
- Breads 6
  - Banana Bread 6
  - Blueberry Bread 8
  - Flax Bread 9
  - Pumpkin Spice Muffins with Flax 10
  - Flax and Orange Muffins 12
  - Berry and Banana Flax Muffins 14
- Soups 15
  - Orzo, Lentil and Flax Soup 15
- Breakfast 17
  - Blueberry, Raisin and Flaxseed Pancakes 17
  - Flaxseed Waffles with Strawberries 19
  - French toast 20
  - Flaxseed and Chocolate Chip Pan Cakes 21
- Snacks 23
  - Hummus 23
  - Banana and Flaxseed Balls 25
  - Flax Seed Crackers 26
  - Flaxseed, Peanut Butter and Oatmeal Cookies 27
  - Granola Snack Bars 28
  - Flax Snacks 29
  - Flaxseed Garlic Bread 31
  - Flaxseed Salsa 32
  - Flaxseed Guacamole 33
  - Flaxseed and Fruit Salsa 34
  - Flaxseed, Artichoke and Spinach Dip 35
  - Flaxseed Cheese Balls 36
  - Flaxseed Spinach Dip 37
- Main Course 38

- Marinated Flaxseed Chicken Kabobs 38
- Grilled Chicken 40
- Black Bean and Flaxseed Burgers 41
- Chicken Pot Pie 43
- Meat Loaf 45
- Flax Porridge 46
- Oven Baked Chicken 47
- Knishes 48

Desserts 50
- Cranberry, Flaxseed and Apple Crisp 50
- Double Chocolate Brownies 52
- Yummy Flaxseed Bonbons 54
- Cinnamon Flax Scones 55
- Peanut Butter Chocolate Chunk Cookies 56
- Crispy Gluten free Shortbread Cookies 58
- Apple and Flaxseed Pie 59

Drinks 60
- Fruit Flax Seed Shake 60
- Flaxseed Smoothies 61
- Mango and Flaxseed Shake 62

Salad and Starters 63
- Flaxseed and Corn Salad 63
- Baked Mushrooms and Potatoes 65
- Flaxseed Green Beans 66
- Flaxseed and Garlic Cauliflower 67
- Asparagus with Balsamic butter and Flaxseed 68
- Mac and Cheese 69

Conclusion: 70

Breads

Banana Bread

Serving Size: 8 person (2 slices each)

Cooking Time: 60-70 Minutes

Ingredients:

1½ cup Gluten free flour (all purpose)

2 Eggs

2 teaspoon of baking powder

4 tablespoon of canola oil

½ teaspoon of table salt

3 tablespoons of raw honey

2-3 medium sized bananas (mashed)

¼ cup of fat free milk

½ teaspoon of vanilla essence

4 tablespoons of walnuts (Chopped)

3 tablespoon full of flaxseed

Process:

Heat the oven to bake the Banana bread at 350°F. Add Gluten free flour (all purpose), raw honey and salt in a mixing bowl. Mix all the ingredients well with help of a spoon and then add baking soda to it and stir.

Take another clean bowl and add mashed bananas, milk, eggs and vanilla essence. With help of a whisk beat all the ingredients until they are united. Now add chopped or crushed walnuts in the mixture. Add Flaxseed and fold all the ingredients together.

Pour the mixture in the Gluten free flour slowly and fold it to make a batter. Keep stirring to avoid formation of any lumps. Take a baking tray for breads and grease it with cooking oil or non-stick spray.

Pour the mixture in the baking pan. Put the pan inside the preheated oven and bake for good 40-50 minutes. Check after 30 minutes by inserting a tooth pick or a knife. If it comes out clean its ready. If not wait until the crust is of light brown in color. Allow the baking dish to cool before taking out the bread. Serve with Tea.

Blueberry Bread

Serving Size: 5-6 Persons

Cooking Time: 35-45 minutes

Ingredients:

4 tablespoons of lemon juice

Half teaspoon of baking soda

¼ cup of oil

½ tablespoon of vanilla essence

4-5 tablespoon of soymilk

4 tablespoon of Flaxseed

1 cup raw honey

1 tablespoon full of baking powder

2 cups Gluten free flour (all purpose)

1 cup Blueberries

Process:

Heat the oven to bake the Blueberry bread at 350°F. Add raw honey vanilla essence, oil, lemon juice and soymilk and stir well. Slowly and bit by bit add the Gluten free flour (all purpose) baking soda and baking powder in the mixture and fold it to make a batter.

When the batter is ready, add the blueberries in it and fold them in the batter. Take baking pan and grease it with oil or non-stick spray. Pour in the batter and with help of spoon stir the blueberries in the tray once again to ensure equal distribution.

Put the pan inside the preheated oven and bake for good 30-40 minutes. Check after 30 minutes by inserting a tooth pick or a knife. If it comes out clean its ready. If not wait until the crust is of light brown in color. Allow the baking dish to cool before slicing.

Flax Bread

Serving Size: 5-6 person

Cooking Time: 20-25 minutes

Ingredients:

1¼ cup of water

4 tablespoons of Flaxseed

2 tablespoons of oil

3 cups Gluten free flour (all purpose)

1½ tablespoon of instant yeast

1 tablespoon of salt

2 tablespoon of honey

Sunflower seeds to dust

Process:

Carefully measure all the ingredients and add them in a clean, dry bowl. Add the dry ingredients in the bowl first and stir them well. Then add the rest of the ingredient and whisk well to make a batter. Make sure you whisk well to avoid formation of any lumps in it.

Preheat the oven at 180C 10-15 minutes before putting the baking dish inside the oven. Take the baking dish and grease it with oil or non-stick spray, whichever do you prefer. Pour the batter gently into the baking dish and level it from the top with help of a spatula.

Put the baking dish inside the oven and bake the bread for 1-25 minutes. Keep checking it after every 10 minutes by inserting a tooth pick in the center. If it comes out clean it is ready. Allow the bread to cool before you slice it.

Pumpkin Spice Muffins with Flax

Serving Size: 24 Medium sized Muffins

Cooking Time: 15-25 minutes

Ingredients:

2 cups of Gluten free flour (all purpose)

1 cup raw honey (powdered)

4 tablespoons off Flaxseeds

2 teaspoons of baking powder

4 tablespoons of Raisins

½ teaspoon salt

1 cup of milk

1 teaspoon of vanilla essence

2 medium sized Eggs

4 tablespoon of Butter

Pumpkin pie mix, 1 can

Process:

Heat the oven for baking muffins at 350 to 400°F. Add Gluten free flour (all purpose), raw honey, salt, Flaxseeds and baking powder in a mixing bowl. Mix all the ingredients well with help of a spoon.

Take another bowl and add eggs, milk and vanilla and whisk well. When they are of uniform consistency add butter (melted and cool, don't pour hot melted butter) in it and mix well.

Pour the batter slowly in the Gluten free flour mixture and stir. Add the pumpkin pie mixture in it and mix slightly. Break any lumps formed during the procedure. Whisk the batter well.

Take a muffin or cupcake baking tray and grease it with cooking oil. Pour the batter in the cups and put the baking tray in the oven. Bake the muffins for good 20 minutes. Check after 10 minutes with a toothpick, if it comes out clean they are ready.

Allow the muffins to cool down a bit before taking them out. Serve with tea.

Flax and Orange Muffins

Serving Size: 16-18 medium sized muffins

Cooking Time: 35-40 minutes

Ingredients:

1½ cup of Bran Oats

1 cup Gluten free flour (all purpose)

4 tablespoons of flaxseed

1 tablespoon of baking powder

Half teaspoon of salt

1½ cup of oranges (cut into pieces and seeds removed)

1 cup of brown or raw honey

1 cup of buttermilk

Half cup of oil

2 large eggs

1 cups raisins

1 teaspoon of baking soda

1 tablespoon of Orange Zest

Process:

Preheat the oven at 350-375° for baking muffins. Take a large clean bowl and add Gluten free flour, bran oats, baking powder, salt and flaxseeds, Mix the ingredients and put them aside. Take another bowl and add eggs, buttermilk, brown raw honey and baking soda. Mix all the ingredients and forma batter. Fold in the orange pieces in it and blend well. Add the batter in the Gluten free flour mixture and keep stirring to avoid formation of lumps. Mix well to form a muffin batter. Now add raisins and mix well.

Take a muffin tray and line it with baking paper. Slightly grease it with cooking oil and pour in muffin batter. Fill the batter to the top, leave only slight space to avoid over flowing.

Put the tray inside the preheated oven bake for 15-20 minutes. Check with help of a tooth pick, if it comes out clean they are ready. Wait for 5-8 minutes before taking out the muffins from tray.

Berry and Banana Flax Muffins

Serving Size: 15-18 Muffins

Cooking Time: 15-20 minutes

Ingredients:

1 egg

1 cup banana (mashed)

1.5 cup rice milk

Half tsp of baking soda

Half cup oats (Quick cooking)

Half cup of raw honey

1 cup Berries

2 tsp pumpkin mix

1 cup Gluten free flour (all purpose)

4 tablespoons Flaxseed

Process:

Preheat the oven at 350-400° for baking. Take a clean bowl and add Oats, wheat, raw honey, salt, pumpkin pie mix and flaxseeds. Mix the ingredients well and keep the bowl aside.

Take another bowl and add eggs, mashed bananas and rice milk. Mix all the ingredients and form a batter. Add the batter in the Gluten free flour mixture and keep stirring to avoid formation of lumps. Mix well until it becomes of uniform consistency.

Now grease the muffin tray with cooking oil, line it with baking paper and pour the batter on the bottom of it. Add fresh and ripe berries and then cover it with batter. Fill the batter to the top, leave only slight space to avoid over flowing.

Put the tray inside the preheated oven bake for 15-20 minutes. Check with help of a tooth pick, if it comes out clean they are ready. Wait for 5-8 minutes before taking out the muffins from tray. Check after 10 minutes with a toothpick, if it comes out clean they are ready. Allow the muffins to cool down a bit before taking them out. Serve with tea.

Soups

Orzo, Lentil and Flax Soup

Serving Size: 10 serving

Cooking Time: 40-50 minutes

Ingredients:

2 tablespoon full of Butter

½ cup finely chopped carrot

½ cup finely chopped Onion

4-5 cups of water

½ cup finely chopped celery stalk

½ cup of chicken stalk (Low sodium)

2 finely chopped green chilies,

2 bay leaves

2 teaspoons of crushed garlic

1.75lbs tomatoes cut into cubes

1½ teaspoon of Worcestershire sauce

½ cup of orzo (Gluten free) pasta

1 teaspoon of crushed raw honey

½ cup of lentils (soaked and rinsed)

2-3 tablespoons of flaxseed

Process:

Heat a large sauce pan on the stove. Add butter in it and melt it. Add the finely chopped vegetables (carrot, onion, chilies, celery) to the pan and sauté the vegetables on low-heat. Do not stir too much, gently stir and cook for about 15-18 minutes or until they are soft and tender.

When the vegetables are tender and soft add the water (make sure it is boiling) to the pan and stir gently. When the water starts boiling again, add the chicken stalk, lentils, garlic, salt, sauce pasta (Gluten free) and tomatoes. Stir gently.

Turn the heat up a bit until the water starts boiling. After 5 minutes, simmer the soup on low heat. Put the lid on and allow the soup to cook and lentils to get soft and tender. Add raw honey and flaxseeds. Stir and serve with freshly chopped basil and parsley

Breakfast

Blueberry, Raisin and Flaxseed Pancakes

Serving Size: 2-3 persons

Cooking Time: 15-20 minutes

Ingredients:

1½ cup soymilk

1 cup Gluten free flour (all purpose)

4 tablespoons Gluten free oat flour

½ cup raisins

Half teaspoon of salt

½ Cup Blueberries

2-3 tablespoons of flaxseed

¼ teaspoon of cinnamon

1-2 teaspoons of oil (For each pancake)

1 cup Maple/chocolate syrup or Honey

4 tablespoons of pastry flour (Gluten free)

1 tablespoon of baking powder

½ cup walnuts or pecans (roasted and chopped finely)

Process:

Take a large bowl and add all the dry ingredients in it except the dry fruits and fruits. Add Gluten free flour, salt, raw honey, baking powder, cinnamon, Gluten free pastry flour, Gluten free oat flour and flaxseed. Stir it with spoon and place it aside.

Add soy milk to it and make a batter. Ensure that there are no lumps in the batter. Remove if any lumps are formed. Add blueberry and raisins in the batter and then stir slightly.

Put a large pan on the stove and add 1-2 teaspoon of oil to grease the surface. Pour the batter on the pan with help of a cup. Make sure you don't use more than ¼ of the cup. Pour the batter in the center allow it to cook until it becomes a bit solid.

Turn sides and see if the other side is golden brown in color. Take out the pancake in a large plate pour maple syrup, honey or chocolate on top and serve with walnuts.

Flaxseed Waffles with Strawberries

Serving Size: 2-3 persons

Cooking Time: 15-25 minutes

Ingredients:

1½ cups pastry flour (Gluten free)

1 tablespoon ground cinnamon

½ teaspoon of cinnamon

4 tablespoons of flaxseed

1 tablespoon of baking powder

2Tablespoon of Raw honey powder

½ teaspoon of Salt

1 tablespoon of oil

1½ cup of milk

Maple/chocolate syrup or Honey

1 tablespoon Vanilla Essence

1 cup sliced strawberries

Process:

Take a bowl and add cinnamon, pastry flour, baking powder, and salt, raw honey, flaxseed and raw honey powder. Mix all the ingredients well with help of a spoon. Add vanilla essence and milk and mix until it forms a batter of uniform consistency.

Check the consistency of the batter it would be lumpy and thick. If it is too lumpy add 3-4 tablespoons of milk and mix well. Pour the waffle batter on the waffle maker and cook for 2-3 minutes. Serve waffles with Strawberries and syrup of your choice.

Pour onto waffle iron and cook according to manufacturer's instructions.

French toast

Serving Size: 2-3 Persons

Cooking Time: 15-20 Minutes

Ingredients:

1 cup of Skimmed milk

½ Eggs

3-4 tablespoons of yeast flakes, nutritional pack

4 teaspoons of powdered raw honey

¼ teaspoon of salt teaspoon salt

½ teaspoon of cinnamon

½ tablespoon of lemon juice

½ teaspoon vanilla essence

1 tablespoon paste of flaxseed (blend flaxseed with water)

5-6 slices of Gluten free bread

Process:

Take a large, clean bowl and add all the ingredients in it. Add milk, cinnamon, lemon juice, raw honey, salt, vanilla essence and yeast flakes. Mix all the ingredients together and make a batter. Keep the batter aside. Take another bowl and whisk the egg. Add half egg in the batter and then beat until the mixture becomes of uniform consistency.

Put a large pan on the stove and pour 1 tablespoon of oil on it. Take one slice at a time and dip it from both sides in the batter. Make sure you don't drench it in it. Just slightly dip it from both sides.

Place the bread slice on the pan. Repeat the procedure with rest of the slices. Allow one side of the bread to turn golden brown and turn sides. Serve the French toast with strawberries or any other fruit of your choice.

Flaxseed and Chocolate Chip Pan Cakes

Serving Size: 2-3 persons

Cooking Time: 15-20 minutes

Ingredients:

1½ cup skimmed milk

1½ cup Gluten free flour

4 tablespoons of Flax seed

½ cup chocolate chips (brown and white)

Half teaspoon of salt

½ teaspoon of cinnamon

1-2 teaspoons of oil (For each pancake)

1 tablespoon of Vanilla Essence

1 cup Chocolate syrup or Honey

1 tablespoon of baking powder

1 tablespoon of icing raw honey (Optional)

Cube of butter (Optional)

1 Cup of Fresh Cream (Optional)

Process:

Take a large bowl and add all the dry ingredients in it fruits and chocolate chips. Add flour, salt, baking powder, cinnamon and flaxseed. Stir it with spoon and place it aside.

Add skimmed milk to it and make a batter. Ensure that there are no lumps in the batter. Remove if any lumps are formed. Add vanilla essence in the batter and mix well.

Put a large pan on the stove and add 1-2 teaspoon of oil to grease the surface. Pour the batter on the pan with help of a cup. Make sure you don't use more than ¼ of the cup. Pour the batter in the center allow it to cook until it becomes a bit solid.

Right before flipping sides, add chocolate chips on the pancake and then flip. Serve hot with chocolate syrup or honey. Decorate with cream, butter and icing raw honey.

Plain Flaxseed Pancakes

Serving Size: 3 persons

Cooking Time: 20 minutes

Ingredients:

2 cup soymilk

2 cup Gluten free flour

1 teaspoon of salt

¾ cup of oil

1 tbsp of Vanilla Essence

1 tbsp of baking powder

1 tbsp of icing raw honey

Maple Syrup

Cube of butter

2-3 tablespoon of Flaxseed

Process:

Take a large bowl add flour, salt and baking powder in it. Mix well and put it aside.

Add soymilk and vanilla essence to the mixture and make a batter Remove the lumps from the batter.

Put a large pan on the stove and add 1 tsp of oil to grease the pan. Pour the batter on the pan. Pour enough to make a small pan cake. Pour the batter in the center slowly so it forms the round cake as you pour it. Serve hot. Decorate with, butter, maple syrup and icing raw honey.

Snacks

Hummus

Serving Size: 2-3 Person

Cooking Time: 10-15

Ingredients:

40 grams of boiled chickpeas

½ cup of chickpea water (boil chickpeas in water)

1 tablespoon of Paprika

4-5 tablespoons of lemon juice

½ teaspoon of cumin powder

4 teaspoons of Tahini Sauce

2 garlic cloves (crushed)

¼ tablespoon of salt

¼ teaspoon of cayenne

¼ teaspoon of pepper

4 teaspoons of Olive Oil

Gluten free French bread (Optional)\Basil leaves (Optional)

2 tbsp Tamari liquid (Optional)

Process:

Soak flaxseeds overnight in a bowl of water and grind them to paste in the morning.

Add boiled chickpeas in a food processor. And blend it. Add lemon juice garlic and Tahini sauce to it and then grind for 12 minutes again. Add other spices like salt, pepper cumin and paprika and then grind some more.

Keep grinding the mixture until it starts to look like a fine and smooth paste. Add one tablespoon of olive oil and flaxseed paste. Grind for just few seconds and then pour the mixture in a bowl. Do not add water to pour it out, use a spoon instead to maintain the thick consistency of the Hummus.

Make a well in the center of the hummus and pour 2-3 tablespoon of olive oil. Decorate it with basil leaves and serve with bread.

Banana and Flaxseed Balls

Serving Size: 8-12 Balls

Cooking Time: 15-25 minutes

Ingredients:

2 tablespoons of Lemon Juice

2-3 tablespoons of Apple (Mashed)

½ cup mashed banana

2 tablespoons butter (Almond butter preferred or you can even take peanut butter)

½ cup of biscuits (Crushed)

½ cup Almonds

1/2 cup of chopped dates

½ cup of coconut powder

3 teaspoons flaxseed

3 tablespoon of chocolate powder

Process:

Add apples, bananas, lemon juice and mix well. Grind the crushed dates, banana and apple mixture and butter and grind well until they all form a pure. Blending will make the mixture to appear liquid like. This is the right consistency.

In another bowl, mix rest of the ingredients with the puree, just not the chocolate powder. Mix all the ingredients well. Fold in 2-3 tablespoons of coconut powder in it. Save the rest for garnishing.

The mixture will be a bit lumpy now take it in hand and start rolling small portions of it into round balls. Roll the balls into the chocolate powder and then into coconut powder. Repeat the procedure with rest of the mixture and refrigerate the balls. Serve cold.

Flax Seed Crackers

Serving Size: 2 per person (24 Crackers)

Cooking Time: 20-25 Minutes

Ingredients:

4 tablespoons of flaxseed

Half teaspoon of baking powder

Half teaspoon of salt

½ teaspoon of cinnamon

4 teaspoon butter, softened

Half cup skimmed milk

1½ cup Gluten free flour (all purpose)

Process:

Preheat the oven at 300 to 325° F. In a bowl take crushed flaxseeds, add other dry ingredients like, raw honey, flour, cinnamon, butter and salt. Take a spatula and mix thoroughly. You can use a mixer if you like. Mix all the ingredients well. The ingredients will start to look like small lumps.

Add milk and again mix well dissolving the lumps in it. Add only enough milk to form dough from the mixture. The dough should be very soft. It is bets if you use hand to knead the dough.

Cover the dough bowl with plastic and put it aside for half an hour or so. After half an hour divide the dough into equal portions. Make 4 equal portions. Shape them in slightly flat rectangles and then cut them into crackers. The cracker should be square preferably.

Take a baking tray and grease it with oil. Transfer the cracker on the baking sheet and place it on the tray/ Put the tray in the preheated oven and bake the cracker for 10-15 minutes.

Flaxseed, Peanut Butter and Oatmeal Cookies

Serving Size: 3-4 person

Cooking Time: 10 minutes

Ingredients:

Half cup of peanut butter

1 cup of Gluten free flour (all purpose)

¾ cup of maple syrup

1 cup raisins

3/4 cup raw honey

½ tablespoon of baking soda

Half teaspoon salt

¾ cup flaxseed

½ cup milk

1 tablespoon of vanilla

3 cups of uncooked oatmeal

Process:

Heat the oven at 375ºF before baking the cookies. Take a bowl and add ingredients like maple syrup, raw honey and peanut butter and beta them well. They will begin to appear a bit creamy. That is the indication that you are doing it right.

Now add flaxseed, vanilla essence and milk in the butter mixture. Mix well and blend if the need be. Take another bowl and mix dry ingredients like baking soda, oatmeal, flour and salt.

Mix all the ingredients. Now add this mixture into peanut butter mixture slowly. Fold the entire mixture in peanut butter mixture and make a paste. Add raisins and mix well.

Take a baking tray and grease it with oil. Now with help of a spoon pour in round cookie dough and spread it to look like a cookie with help of a spoon. Don't press too much. Put the baking tray inside the preheated oven bake the cookies for 5-8 minutes.

Granola Snack Bars

Serving Size: 45-50 bars

Cooking Time: 30-35 minutes

Ingredients:

0.25 lbs Butter

2 cups Marshmallows (Mini)

5 tablespoons of flaxseed

½ cup of chopped Raisins

2 tablespoons of Sunflower Seeds (Raw and shelled)

3-4 tablespoons of Grated coconut

0.5 lbs Crackers (Crushed)

0.35 lbs Oats (Rolled)

Process:

Take a saucepan and add butter in it. Melt the butter on low to medium heat. Make sure you don't burn the butter. Add one teaspoon of cooking oil to prevent the butter from getting burned.

Now add the mini marshmallows to the butter and stir with a wooden spatula or spoon. Stir gently and until they are smooth and melted. Put the saucepan aside. Now add crunchy ingredients like oats, cracker crumbs, flaxseeds, raisins and grated coconut. Fold all the ingredients in the butter and marshmallow mixture.

Take a baking dish and grease it with cooking oil or butter then pour the mixture on the tray. It will be bit thick. Press and spread it across the length of the tray. Make sure you don't press it too much else the bars will be too thin. Allow the mixture to cool and then cut it into bars.

Flax Snacks

Serving Size: 4-8 Person

Cooking Time: 10-15 minutes

Ingredients:

1 cup corn syrup

6 cups of Rice Crispies

10 tablespoons of brown raw honey

5-6 tablespoons of Flaxseeds

½ tablespoon of vanilla essence

8 tablespoon full of peanut butter

Process:

Add all the ingredients in a bowl except rise crispies. Mix all the ingredients well. Take a sauce pan and heat over low flame. Add the mixture in it and melt it. Now add rice crispies to the melted and smooth mixture and stir well. Take the sauce pan off of the flame and put it aside

Grease a baking tray with butter or cooking oil and pour the mixture on it. Spread in the tray. Make a thick layer and allow it to cool. And then cut it into 8 bars.

Apple Crisp

Serving Size: 8 person

Cooking Time: 40-50 Minutes

Ingredients:

2 teaspoon of lemon juice

4 tablespoon of raw honey (crushed to powder)

4 tablespoon of flaxseed

3 tablespoon full of brown raw honey

4 tablespoon of Oats (Instant to cook)

1tablespoon of cinnamon powder

3 large sliced apples

2 teaspoons of Gluten free flour mix

Process:

Heat the oven at 350 °F. Tale a baking dish and place the sliced apples on it. Pour the lemon juice and coat the sliced apples in it.

Take another bowl and add Gluten free flour mix, 2 tablespoon of raw honey and 1 tablespoon of cinnamon in it. Mix well. Sprinkle the dry mixture on the sliced apples in the baking tray and coat the sliced apples well.

Now take another bowl and add the rest of the raw honey, cinnamon and oats with flaxseeds and mix well. Now Sprinkle this mixture too on all the apples. Don't toss and don't move the apples now.

Put the baking tray in the preheated oven. Bake the apples until they are crisp, or for at least 30-40 minutes. Make sure you don't overcook and burn the crisp.

Take out when the crisp is golden brown and serve with ice cream or fresh cream.

Flaxseed Garlic Bread

Serving Size: 10 Person

Cooking Time: 15 Minutes

Ingredients:

1 lbs loaf of Gluten free Italian bread

5 tbsp softened butter,

2 tsp olive oil

1 tbsp crushed garlic,

1 tsp crushed oregano

2 tbsp of Flaxseed (crushed)

Salt to taste

Pepper to taste

1 cup mozzarella cheese (grated and gluten free)

Process:

Heat the oven at 350F. Cut thick slices of the French loaf. Mix all the ingredients except cheese in a bowl and form a mixture. Apply the mixture on the garlic bread. Take a baking tray and place baking paper on it. Place all the garlic breads on the tray ad place the tray in the preheated oven for 10 minutes. Apply the cheese on top of all the breads and bake until the cheese melts. Serve hot.

Flaxseed Salsa

Serving Size: 16 Person

Cooking Time: 10 Minutes

Ingredients:

1lb of tomatoes (stewed)

Half onion, (chopped)

1 tsp of garlic (chopped)

Half lemon's juice

1 tsp of salt

1½ tbsp of Flaxseed, powdered

1/4 cup of green chilies (chopped)

3 tbsp chopped cilantro

Process:

Add all the ingredients in a blender and blend for 30 seconds. Blend until the desired consistency is achieved.

Flaxseed Guacamole

Serving Size: 4 person

Cooking Time: 10 Minutes

Ingredients:

3 avocados (cut into small squares)

1 lemon's juice

1 tsp salt or to taste

Half a cup of onion (chopped)

3 tbsp cilantro (chopped)

2 plum tomatoes, (chopped)

1 tsp garlic, (chopped)

1 tbsp of Flaxseed (powdered and crushed)

Process:

Take bowl and add tomatoes, avocados, lemon juice, flaxseed powder and salt. Mix all the ingredients together and blend well. Now add onion, cilantro and garlic and mix in the avocado mixture. Put the mixture in the refrigerator. Serve as a dip.

Flaxseed and Fruit Salsa

Serving Size: 10 person

Cooking Time: 45 Minutes

Ingredients:

2 kiwis (cut into small squares)

2 apples (cut into small squares)

0.5 lbs raspberries (cut into pieces)

1 lb strawberries (cut into pieces)

2 tbsp raw honey (powdered)

1 tbsp brown raw honey

2 tbsp cinnamon raw honey

3 tbsp fruit preservatives

2 Tbsp of Flaxseed

10 Gluten free flour tortillas

Cooking spray

Process:

In large bowl add all the fruits chopped into small pieces, flaxseed and mix with wooden spoons. Don't mix the ingredients too well or the salsa will appear messy. Now add fruits preservatives and raw honeys. Mix well. Put the fruits in the refrigerator

Heat the oven at 350F. In the mean while spray the tortillas with cooking spray. Sprinkle cinnamon on it. Spray the tortillas again with the cooking spray and place the tortillas on a baking tray and put it in the preheated oven. Bake the tortillas for 5 minutes and then serve with the chilled Salsa.

Flaxseed, Artichoke and Spinach Dip

Serving Size: 4 Person

Cooking Time: 45 minutes

Ingredients:

1 lb artichokes cut into small pieces

1/3 cup Romano cheese, (grated and Gluten free)

1/4 cup Parmesan cheese, (grated and Gluten free)

Half tsp garlic (Chopped)

0.85 spinach, chopped

2 tablespoons of Flaxseed

1/3 cup cream

Half a cup of sour cream

1 cup mozzarella cheese (shredded and Gluten free)

Process:

Heat the oven at 350F. Grease a baking dish and put aside. Blend all the ingredients except, cream, spinach, and cheese in a blender. Mix until all the ingredients form a mixture and are chopped well.

In another bowl make a mixture of cream, spinach, and cheese. Now add the mixture of artichoke in it and mix well. Pour the mixture in the baking dish and put it in the preheated oven for baking. Bake it for 20 minutes or until the crust is of golden brown in color.

Flaxseed Cheese Balls

Serving Size: 5-6 person

Cooking Time: 20 minutes

Ingredients:

0.5 lbs cream cheese (Gluten free)

0.5 lbs pineapple, cut into pieces

1 tbsp onion (chopped)

1 tbsp bell pepper (chopped)

1/4 tbsp salt

1 cup roasted pecans (chopped)

2 tablespoon of Flaxseed

Process:

Take bowl and mix all the ingredients together except the flaxseed and pecans. Make a soft mixture of all the ingredients. Make small balls. In a plate, mix flaxseed and roasted pecans. Roll the cheese balls in the mixture. Serve with tea or smoothie.

Flaxseed Spinach Dip

Serving Size:

Cooking Time:

Ingredients:

0.25 lbs vegetable soup mix

1 lbs sour cream

0.62 lbs spinach, chopped

1 tablespoon of flaxseed

1 lbs loaf pumpernickel (Gluten free)

Process:

Take a bowl and add chopped spinach, cream and soup mix and mix all the ingredients well. Trim the pumper nickels loaf from top and sides and make a bread bowl of it. Serve the spinach dip in the bowl made of the loaf. Serve with tortillas and nachos.

Main Course

Marinated Flaxseed Chicken Kabobs

Serving Size: 8 Person

Cooking Time: 45 Minutes

Ingredients:

0.5lbs plain yogurt (no fat)

Half a cup of feta cheese (crumbled and Gluten free)

3 tablespoons of basil

1 cup of sun-dried tomatoes

Half a tsp of lemon zest

2 tbsp lemon juice

2 tsp oregano (crushed)

1 ½ tbsp of flaxseed (crushed into powder

Half a tsp salt

Half a tsp black pepper (freshly crushed)

Half a tsp rosemary (dried and crushed)

1 lbs boneless chicken breast (cut into 1 inch cubes)

1 red onion (cut in squares)

1 green bell pepper or capsicum (cut in squares) one and a half inch pieces

Process

Take a bowl and make a mixture of rosemary, salt, pepper, flaxseed powder, yogurt, cheese, and lemon juice, and mix all the ingredients. Place the chicken pieces in the bowl and coat well in the mixture you made. Allow the chicken to absorb all the flavors. Put the chicken to marinate aside for 2-3 hours.

Heat the grill in the meanwhile to grill the kabobs. Place the chicken and vegetables on the skewers and place them on the grill. Allow one side to get grilled and then turn on other. Serve with your favorite sauce.

Grilled Chicken

Serving Size:

Cooking Time:

Ingredients:

4 chicken breast, Halved

Half a cup of lemon juice

Half a tsp onion powder

Black pepper to taste (Freshly crushed)

Salt to taste

2 tsp parsley (dried and crushed)

2 tbsp of Flaxseed (Crushed and powdered

Process

Prepare the grill for grilling the chicken. In the mean while Take a bowl and add lemon juice, flaxseed powder, parsley and lemon juice in it and coat the chicken well. Now sprinkle salt and pepper and allow the chicken to absorb the flavor for half an hour.

Place the marinated chicken on the grill and allow it to get cooked. Grill on both sides until no pink color is left. Serve with Gluten free bread and dip.

Black Bean and Flaxseed Burgers

Serving Size: 2-3 person

Cooking Time: 30 Minutes

Ingredients:

3 cups cooked black beans (You can opt for canned black beans if you want)

4 tablespoons of walnuts (chopped)

4-5 tablespoons of carrots (grated)

2 teaspoons of (Gluten free) soy sauce

2 teaspoons of water

½ teaspoon of table salt

1 tablespoon of basil leaves (crushed)

1 teaspoon of oregano

1 teaspoon of onion powder

½ teaspoon of black pepper

½ tablespoons of red pepper

4-5 tablespoon of flaxseed (crushed)

Mayonnaise (Optional)

HP sauce (Optional)

Ketchup (Optional)

Mustard paste (Optional)

Lettuce leaves and sliced tomatoes (Optional)

Process:

Take bowl and add black beans t it. Mash it with help of a spoon. Add rest of the ingredients in the mashed beans and mix well. Make sure all the ingredients are mixed in the mashed beans well.

At times the mixture might appear a bit dry to make the patties. Add I tablespoon of olive oil or 2 tablespoon of water to make it a bit soft. Divide the mixture into equal portions and make round patties for the burger.

Take a skillet and grease it with oil, add about 4-5 tablespoon of cooking or olive oil (whichever you prefer the most) place the patties in the skillet. Don't over crowd the skillet. You might break the patties this way. Make sure you have enough space in the skillet to turn and move the patties. Cook from one side for 3-4 minutes and then carefully turn the side.

Apply mayonnaise, HP sauce and mustard paste. Place lettuce leaves and tomatoes. Carefully place the Pattie and your burger is ready to eat!

Chicken Pot Pie

Serving Size: 2-3 Person

Cooking Time: 2.5 Hours

Ingredients:

8 pieces boneless chicken (2lbs)

4 cups Chicken Stock (low sodium and Gluten free)

1 cup onion (1.5 medium onions)

2 stalks of celery, (Chopped into small squares)

1-2 bay leaves

¼ tablespoon of black pepper

Half a cup of cold water

¼ cup Gluten free flour (all purpose)

1 cup of vegetables (Freshly cut)

3 tablespoon of flaxseed

1 pie crust (Freshly made and according to the size of your pie pot)

Process:

Heat the oven at 350-370 ° F, 15 minutes before baking the pot pie. Take a pan and add chicken stock, bay leaves, and other vegetables. Let them come to boil. Add pepper and chicken to the pan. Now let the chicken and vegetables to get tender in chicken stock. Put a lid on the pan and let the mixture cook for about 1.5 hours.

Check, when the chicken is tender. Take the pan off of the stove. Put it aside. Allow the mixture to cool a bit and then extract the vegetables and chicken from the stock. Store the stock in a bowl.

Take a small cup and dissolve the flour in the water. Make sure it is not either too thick or too thin. It should be of medium consistency. Add the mixture in the stock and keep stirring. This will make the stock get a bit thick.

Add the chicken, flaxseeds and vegetables into the mixture and then cook for 5-10 more minutes. Distribute the prepared mixture in 4 small pots. Cover the pots or cups with the pie crust. Apply a little butter on top and place the cups in the preheated oven for 10 15 minutes. Take out and then serve hot. Place mixture into 4 individual baking dishes (coated with non-stick spray).

Meat Loaf

Serving Size: 4-8 person

Cooking Time: 2 Hours

Ingredients:

0.9 Kg beef (lean)

¼ tablespoon of celery salt

1 cup of fat free milk

¾ cup Gluten free bread crumbs

2 medium onions (Chopped)

4 tablespoon of flaxseed

1 Egg

5 tablespoon of tomato ketchup

½ tablespoon of black pepper

½ tablespoon of dry mustard

1 tablespoon of Worcestershire sauce

½ tablespoon of garlic powder

¼ teaspoon thyme

Process:

Heat the oven for baking the loaf at 350ºF. Take a bowl and add beef, flaxseed, bread crumbs, Worcestershire sauce, egg, onion, mustard, salt, thyme and garlic. Mix all the ingredients well and cover the beef in the mixture.

Take a loaf pan and put the loaf and the mixture in it. Settle all the ingredients in one level with help of a spoon. Pour the ketchup on top of the loaf. Pout the loaf in the oven and bake it for one and a half hour. Bake it until all the pink beef in turned into bit darker shade. It also depends on your taste if you want to cook it 'well done' then bake it for a bit longer.

Take it out of the pan and allow it to settle. Slice and then serve hot.

Flax Porridge

Serving Size: 2-3 person

Cooking Time: 10-15 minutes

Ingredients:

4 cups of water

4 tablespoon of flaxseed

1½ cup of Instant oats

1 Banna (Sliced)

Half cup of Blackcurrant

¼ tablespoon of cinnamon

Process:

Take a sauce pan and pour 4 cups of water in it. Allow it to boil than add oats in it. Keep stirring until it forms a mixture. Add cinnamon and put a lid on the sauce pan and allow the oats to be cooked for 2-3 minutes.

After 2-3 minutes take off the lid and add blackcurrants stir a bit and add flaxseeds. Pour the Porridge in a bowl and pour a bit of a maple syrup, and sliced bananas on top of it.

Oven Baked Chicken

Serving Size:

Cooking Time:

Ingredients:

4 chicken breasts (Boneless)

¼ teaspoon garlic powder

Olive oil

1 cup of Gluten free Bread crumbs

¼ tablespoon of black pepper

1 tablespoon of freshly chopped parsley

2 tablespoon of Parmesan cheese (Gluten free)

¼ teaspoon seasoning

4 tablespoons of flaxseed

Process:

Clean chicken with water. Take pieces of chicken and grease them in olive oil. To coat the chicken breasts, take a bowl and add crumbs, flaxseeds, black pepper, parmesan cheese seasoning (salt) and garlic powder. Mix all the ingredients well. Put the oil glazed chicken in the mixture and coat well.

Take a baking dish and grease it slightly with the olive oil and put the chicken coated in the mixture. Put the dish in the oven to bake the chicken for about 20 to 25 minutes. Different oven takes different time to cook. Keep checking your chicken take it out when it is golden brown in color.

Knishes

Serving Size: 7-8 Person

Cooking Time: 1 hour

Ingredients:

4 cups of potatoes (Mashed)

2-3 tablespoon salt

6 tablespoons flaxseed

2 cup of Gluten free flour

1Cup of Gluten free flour (all purpose)

2 tablespoons cooking oil

7 tablespoons cold water

2 cups onions (Chopped)

1 tablespoon olive oil

½ black pepper

Process:

Take a large bowl; add the 1½ cup of mashed potatoes, 3 tbsp Flaxseed and half a tablespoon of salt. Mix them well and add cooking oil, flours and water. Mix all the ingredients well and put them aside. Heat the onions to bake the knishes at 350°F.

Filling:

Pour olive oil in a pan and sate the onions in it until they change their color to golden brown. Add the onions in a bowl, 2 tbsp, 2½ cups mashed potatoes, salt and pepper. Mix them well.

Take the dough and divide it into 2 equal portions. Roll them out in rectangle and then level the edges by cutting them with knife. Place good amount of filling in the center of the dough and fold up the ends and make a cone look alike and pinch it to seal the knish.

Take a baking dish and grease it slightly with the olive oil and put the knish in the tray. Put the dish in the oven to bake for about 20 to 25 minutes. Different oven takes different time to cook. Keep checking your knishes; take them out when it is golden brown in color.

Desserts

Cranberry, Flaxseed and Apple Crisp

Serving Size: 7-8 Person

Cooking Time: 40-50 minutes

Ingredients:

2-3 apples (Sliced)

1 cup cranberries (Fresh preferred)

5 teaspoon of Apple Cider

2 teaspoons of raw honey

Half a cup of Gluten free flour (all purpose)

1-2 tablespoon of Gluten free flour (all purpose), (Bleached) 4Tablespoon of flaxseed

4-5 Tablespoon of walnuts (chopped)

3 teaspoon of wheat germ

¼ tablespoon of cinnamon

6 teaspoon of cooking oil

Process:

Heat the oven at 375°F for baking the crisp. Take a bowl and add 1 tablespoon of flour raw honey, apples, cider, cranberries and mix well all the ingredients.

Take another bowl and add rest of the flour, brown raw honey, walnuts and wheat germs in it. Mix well. Mix until the mixture starts to appear like crumbs. Sprinkle the dry mixture on the sliced apples in the baking tray and coat the sliced apples well.

Now take another bowl and add the rest of the raw honey, cinnamon and oats with flaxseeds and mix well. Now Sprinkle this mixture too on all the apples. Don't toss and don't move the apples now.

Put the baking tray in the preheated oven. Bake the apples until they are crisp, or for at least 30-40 minutes. Make sure you don't overcook and burn the crisp. Take out when the crisp is golden brown and serve with ice cream or fresh cream.

You can try using other fruits instead of cranberries like, raspberries, bananas and peaches.

Double Chocolate Brownies

Serving Size: 30-40 minutes

Cooking Time:

Ingredients:

Half a cup of cocoa powder

1 cup of Gluten free flour (all purpose)

Half teaspoon of baking soda

1 cup of raw honey (White)

¼ teaspoon of salt

Half a cup tofu (Soft)

Half a cup of water

1 teaspoon vanilla essence

4 tablespoons of flaxseed

1 cup of chocolate chips

4-5 tablespoon of chopped walnuts

4 teaspoons of cooking oil

Process:

Heat the oven at 375°F for baking the crisp. Take a bowl and add cocoa powder, flour, baking soda, raw honey and salt and mix well all the ingredients.

Take another bowl and add soft tofu, flaxseeds, vanilla and water and mix all the ingredients well with help of a spatula or you can always you a blender. Blend or mix until they are extremely smooth.

Divide the chocolate chips in two equal halves and melt one portion of it. Add this melted chocolate to the tofu mixture and blend well. Now stir this puree into the cocoa powder and flour mixture. When all the ingredients are mixed together nicely, fold in the remaining half cup of chocolate chips in the mixture and mix gently. Add the cooking oil in the mixture and again mix well. Remove the air bubbles if any.

Take a baking dish and grease it with butter then sprinkle a bit of flour and toss it in the baking dish. Pour all the batter in the baking dish and level the surface. Place the baking dish in the preheated oven and bake it for good 30-35 minutes.

Take out from the oven and cut the slices immediately. Then allow the brownie to cool down a bit. Serve with chocolate syrup and fruits.

Yummy Flaxseed Bonbons

Serving Size: 100 bonbons

Cooking Time: 40-50 minutes

Ingredients:

1 cup of softened grass fed butter or butter

2 lbs confectioners' raw honey, sifted

0.8 lbs condensed milk (sweetened)

3 cups of coconut (crushed)

2 tbsp of shortening

2 tablespoons of Flaxseed

1 cup of walnuts (coarsely chopped)

1 tsp vanilla essence

0.75 lbs chocolate chips (sweet or semisweet as per your taste)

Process:

Take a large bowl and add butter, condensed milk, raw honey, flaxseed, coconut powder, vanilla essence and chopped walnuts. Mix all the ingredients and put the bowl in the refrigerator and allow the mixture to cool. Refrigerate it until it is hard enough to roll into balls.

Take it out and then roll into hard balls. Don't press to hard. Roll the mixture into balls with help of gentle hands. Place these balls on a butter paper in a tray and place them back in the refrigerator.

Melt chocolate chips and shortening in a double boiler. Take out the bonbons and dip the bonbons on the chocolate and shortening mixture and place it back on the butter paper. Allow them to dry and chocolate to get settles. Place in the small butter cups and serve cold.

Cinnamon Flax Scones

Serving Size: 8 scones

Cooking Time: 40 minutes

Ingredients:

2 cups of Gluten free flour (all purpose)

4 tablespoons of cup raw honey (powdered and crushed)

2 tablespoons of Cinnamon powder + 3 tablespoon

Half a tablespoon of baking powder

1/4 tsp baking soda

Half a tsp salt

Half a cup of butter, (frozen and unsalted)

Half cup of dried currants

Half cup of sour cream

1 egg (whisked)

Process:

Heat an oven for baking the crispy Gluten free short bread cookies at 400°F. Place an oven rack in the oven to bake scones.

In a bowl, add flour, 4 tablespoons of raw honey, and 3 tablespoon of cinnamon salt, baking soda and powder. Add butter in flour mixture and with help of a fork mix the butter coarsely in the flour. It will start to look like a crumble. Now add dry currants or raisins if you like then stir in raisins.

Now beat eggs and cream in another bowl until they form a smooth mixture. Now add this mixture in the flour and butter mixture. With help of a fork mix all the ingredients well and make dough. Mix the dough with hands and knead it to form a perfect ball.

On a clean board sprinkle some flour and spread the dough in a round circle. Or you can make several small round circles. Depends upon the size you want of the cinnamon scones. Sprinkle the cinnamon on top and place the scones on a greased tray. Put the tray in the preheated oven and then bake the scones of 15-20 minutes.

Peanut Butter Chocolate Chunk Cookies

Serving Size: 2 Dozen Cookies

Cooking Time: 30 Minutes

Ingredients:

Half a cup of softened butter

Half a cup of peanut butter

1 cup packed brown raw honey

1 ½ tablespoon of Flaxseed

Half a cup of raw honey

2 eggs, Whisked

2 tbsp corn syrup

2 tbsp water

2 tsp vanilla essence

2.5 cups of Gluten free flour (all purpose)

1 tsp baking soda

Half a tsp salt

2 cups of chopped chocolate or you can use chocolate chips

Process:

Heat an oven for baking the crispy Gluten free short bread cookies at 375°F. Take a clean bowl and add butter and peanut butter in it and beat well. Use an electric beater for best results. Keep whisking the butter until it is soft and fluffy. Now add white and brown raw honey and flaxseed in it, pouring one tablespoon of raw honey at a time. Keep whisking until the butter forms a mixture with raw honey.

Now add water, vanilla essence and corn syrup beat again for a few minutes. Pour in flour, salt and baking soda and use the electric beater to mix it in the butter mixture. Add half a cup at a time. When you are done mixing, add the chocolate chunks or chocolate chip cookies in the dough, mix gently.

Grease a baking tray and put the dough in the tray with help of a spoon. Press a bit to shape the cookie. Now put the tray inside the oven and bake for 10 minutes.

Crispy Gluten free Shortbread Cookies

Serving Size: 2 Dozen Cookies

Cooking Time: 30 Minutes

Ingredients:

2 cups softened butter,

1 ½ tablespoon of Flaxseed

1 cup of raw honey (powdered)

2 tsp vanilla essence

4 cups of Gluten free flour (all purpose)

Process:

Heat an oven for baking the crispy short bread cookies at 350°F. Take a clean bowl and add butter in it and beat well. Use an electric beater for best results. Keep whisking the butter until it is soft and fluffy. Now add raw honey and flaxseed in it, pouring one tablespoon of raw honey at a time. Keep whisking until the butter forms a mixture with raw honey.

Now add vanilla essence beat again for a few minutes. Pour in flour and use the electric beater to mix it in the butter mixture. Add half a cup at a time. Grease a baking tray and put the dough in the tray with help of a spoon. Press a bit to shape the cookie. Now put the tray inside the oven and bake for 10 minutes.

Apple and Flaxseed Pie

Serving Size: 8-9 Person

Cooking Time: 1-1.5Hour

Ingredients:

Half a dozen of apples (cut into cubes)

¼ Tbsp of Powdered nutmeg

5-6 Tbsp of Gluten free flour (all purpose)

4-5 tbsp of Butter

4 cups of raw honey, divided

1 Piecrust (Frozen)

1 tbsp of vanilla essence

Half cup of r Chopped and toasted walnuts, (Optional)

Process:

Heat the oven at 475° for baking the pie. Take a bowl and add sliced apples in it with, 3 cups of raw honey, nutmeg powder and flour. Now put all the ingredients in the pan. Put the pan on the stove and bring the ingredients to boil.

When it starts to bubbles, take the pan off of the stove and add butter and vanilla essence in the mixture and stir well. Take the mixture and put it in the pan baking tray. Fill the baking dish with the mixture till the top. Leave a little bit of space on top. Roll the pie crusts according to the size of the baking tray.

Mix the roasted walnuts in the pie mixture and then sprinkle the remaining raw honey on it. Place the pie crust on top of the baking dish. Seal the sides and place the baking dish in the oven for 25 minutes or until the crust is slightly brown in color. Serve with cream

Drinks

Fruit Flax Seed Shake

Serving Size: 5 minutes

Cooking Time: 2-3 Glass

Ingredients:

0.2 Liter milk (Skimmed milk if you are on diet)

Half cup of Strawberries

Half cup of Raspberries

Half cup of Blueberries

2 Bananas

2 teaspoons of honey

3-4 teaspoons of flaxseed

Process:

Put the ingredients in a blender, except the ice cubes. Blend all the ingredients well until it appears like a fine milkshake. Add Ice cubes, if you are using frozen fruits than Ice cubes will not be required. Blend for 30 seconds and then pour the Fruit Juice in a glass.

Flaxseed Smoothies

Serving Size: 2 Servings

Cooking Time: 5-10 Minutes

Ingredients:

1 banana or 1 cup of /Apples/Raspberries

1½ teaspoon of olive oil

6-7 strawberries

2 teaspoon of raw honey syrup or maple syrup

1 cup of milk

¼ tablespoon of Vanilla essence

2 teaspoons of flaxseed

1-2 cups of Ice cubes

Process:

Pour all the ingredients at once and blend well until the ice and fruits combine to form a puree. Make sure the ice is crushed thoroughly. Take a glass and drizzle some strawberry or maple syrup on it walls. Pour in the smoothie and serve chilled.

You can add other ingredients to develop your taste. You can add a scoop of vanilla ice cream or any other ice cream of your choice for flavor.

It is advised that for enhanced flavor use fresh fruits. Frozen fruits should be avoided. If you don't like your smoothie to be very rich then add just one or half banana.

Mango and Flaxseed Shake

Serving Size: 5 minutes

Cooking Time: 2-3 Glass

Ingredients:

0.5 Liter milk

1 cup of Mango (cut into cubes)

1 cup of Ice cubes

4 Scoops of Mango ice cream

3-4 teaspoons of flaxseed

Process:

Put the ice cubes in a blender and crush them. Now add milk, mango and flaxseed and blend all the ingredients well until it appears like a fine milkshake. Put the Ice cream shake in the glass and pour the milkshake on top of it.

Salad and Starters

Flaxseed and Corn Salad

Serving Size: 4 person

Cooking Time: 20 Minutes

Ingredients:

1 tsp butter

2 cups of corn, boiled

Half red onion, chopped coarsely

2 Tablespoon of Flaxseed

1 tbsp parsley (fresh)

Salt to taste

Black pepper to taste

2 Tablespoon of Flaxseed

1 tbsp fresh chives (chopped)

Half lbs of Shrimps

2 Tablespoon of Lemon Juice

1 tablespoon Italian seasoning

2 Tablespoon of Paprika

2 Tablespoon of Oil

Process:

Take a pan and melt butter in it. Add one tablespoon of cooking oil in it from preventing the butter to burn. Fry the onions until they are soft now add corn and mix them well. Cook the corn and onion for 10 minutes then take them out in a salad bowl. Add parsley and season it with salt and pepper

Take a frying pan and put 2 tablespoon of oil and heat. Marinate shrimps with Italian seasoning, lemon juice, flaxseed powder and paprika. Fry them in the heated oil until they are tender. Take them out in a platter. And serve with corn salad sprinkled with chives on top.

Baked Mushrooms and Potatoes

Serving Size: 4 person

Cooking Time: 45 Minutes

Ingredients:

1 lb of new potatoes, cut into half

2 tbsp olive oil

Half lbs of Portobello mushrooms (sliced)

6 cloves garlic (unpeeled)

2 tbsp thyme (Freshly chopped)

1 tbsp olive oil

2 Tbsp of Flaxseed

Salt and black pepper to taste

6 oz of cherry tomatoes

2 tbsp pine nuts (Roasted)

6 oz of spinach, coarsely chopped

Process:

Heat the oven at 400F. Put a large pan on heat and pour oil in it. Add the halved potatoes in it and sauté for about 15-20 minutes. Keep turning and tossing the potatoes.

Now add the mushrooms in the pan and stir gently. Add garlic to the pan and stir. Season the potatoes with salt, pepper and thyme. Now pour some more olive oil, flaxseed and sauté all the ingredients for 10 minutes.

Grease a baking dish and pour the mushroom and potato mixture in it and put it inside the preheated oven to bake. For 5 minutes. Take it out and add the cherry tomatoes mix all the ingredients and return the dish back to oven cook for 10 minutes/

Remove pan from oven and add spinach and cherry tomatoes. Return to oven, cook until the tomatoes are tender. Sprinkle nuts on top and serve hot.

Flaxseed Green Beans

Serving Size: 5 person

Cooking Time: 25 Minutes

Ingredients:

1 tbsp butter

3 tbsp olive oil

5-6 garlic cloves peeled, crushed and chopped

2 Tbsp of Flaxseed

1 lb green beans

Salt and pepper to taste

1/4 cup Parmesan cheese (grated and Gluten free)

Process:

Heat the oil in a large pan and add butter in it. Now add the chopped garlic and sauté it in the butter over medium heat. Allow the garlic to cook well and change the color to crisp golden brown.

Now add the green beans and season them with pepper and salt. Sauté those in the butter and cook until the beans get soft and tender. Toss, stir and add flaxseed in the pan. Take out the beans and serve with parmesan cheese on top

Flaxseed and Garlic Cauliflower

Serving Size: 6 Person

Cooking Time: 40 Minutes

Ingredients:

2 tbsp garlic (chopped)

3 tbsp olive oil

2 tablespoon of Flaxseed

1 cauliflower, cut into florets

1/3 cup Parmesan cheese (grated and Gluten free)

Salt According to taste

Pepper To taste

1 tbsp parsley (chopped)

Process:

Heat the oven at 450F. Take a baking dish and grease it with nonstick spray or with oil and butter. Take a bowl and mix cauliflower with garlic, flaxseed and olive oil. Keep the cauliflower aside and allow the mixture to absorb its flavor in the cauliflower. Now Add salt and pepper and mix well.

Place the cauliflower mixture in the baking dish and bake them for about 20 minutes then add parmesan cheese on top of it and then bake for another 15 minutes. Bake until the cauliflower is of golden brown in color.

Asparagus with Balsamic butter and Flaxseed

Serving Size: 4 Person

Cooking Time: 25 Minutes

Ingredients:

1 asparagus bunch, cut into 3 inch pieces and trimmed

No-stick Cooking spray

Salt to taste

Pepper to taste

1 tablespoon of Flaxseed (crushed and powdered)

2 tbsp of butter

1 tbsp (Gluten free) soy sauce

1 tsp vinegar (balsamic)

Process:

Heat the oven at 450F. Take a baking dish and place the trimmed, clean, and cut asparagus in the dish. Spray the cooking oil and sprinkle pepper, Flaxseed and salt. Put the asparagus tray in the preheated oven and bake for 10-15 minutes. Check after 10 minutes, if they are tender then take them out else, bake them until they are tender. Melt butter in a pan and add vinegar and (Gluten free) soy sauce in it. Mix well. Pour the butter mixture on top of the asparagus and bake for another 5 minutes. Serve hot.

Mac and Cheese

Serving Size: 6 Persons

Cooking Time: 50 Minutes

Ingredients:

0.5 lbs macaroni (elbow)

0.5 lbs Cheddar cheese (grated)

0.75 lbs cottage cheese (Gluten free)

0.5 lbs sour cream

¼ cup Parmesan cheese (grated and Gluten free)

Salt and pepper (according to taste)

1 cup of Gluten free bread crumbs

1/4 cup of butter

Process:

Heat the oven at 350F. Boil the elbow macaroni according to the instruction of the packet. Boil the macaroni, drain and put them aside.

In a baking dish add cream, cottage cheese, macaroni and parmesan cheese and mix all the ingredients well. Now add melted butter, bread crumbs, pepper and salt and sprinkle it on top of macaroni. Place the dish in the preheated oven and bake for 20-25 minutes.

Conclusion:

Flaxseed has a little too many benefits to ignore and if you are a fan of healthy living and eating this book will help you in creating scrumptious food with healthy ingredients and of course it will enlighten you how you can add Flaxseed into recipes you love while keeping it healthy! Happy eating!

Made in the USA
Middletown, DE
25 April 2024

53476723R00040